CW00766294

Jim Downes
Berthold Daum

The Ghan

From Adelaide to Alice

First published in 1996 by
lichtbild pty ltd
LPO Box 6011
Cromer, Vic 3193
Australia

phone: (03) 9584 9638
email: 100026.3365@compuserve.com

Printed in Australia by Southbank Book

Copyright ©Berthold Daum
Afghan cameleers : ©Christine Stevens
Aborigines and the Ghan Train: ©Dick Kimber
A miner's story: Adapted from *The Silent Partners* ©Margaret Mackay
Tarcoola - The Race-Course: ©Rolly St.Clair
I am at Deep Well: ©The Estate of Roland Robinson
All other text: ©Jim Downes
Copyright of the following images: ©Australian National
p7, p12 top, p12 right, p26 left, p27 right
Copyright all other images ©Berthold Daum

National library of Australia
Cataloguing-in-Publication data:

Downes, J. (Jim), 1934 –
Daum, B. (Berthold), 1949 –

lichtbild

Contents

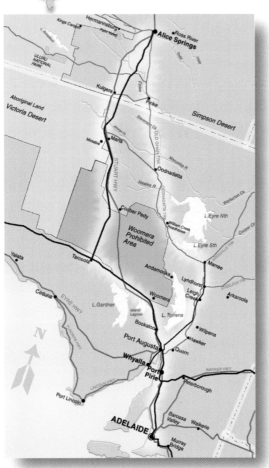

O n a Sunday morning in August, 1929, a mixed passenger and goods train steamed out of Adelaide railway station and through the sparse northern suburbs. Its destination was a thousand miles away, at the centre of Australia, and it carried, as well as more than a hundred through passengers, mail and fresh fruit.

Train day at Stuart: An early Ghan arrives at the tiny railway town which later became "The Alice"

6

This was the first train to Alice Springs, and it arrived, more or less on time, two days later. Railway legend has it that somewhere along the track to the Alice the train lost its official designation, something as prosaic as 'The Alice Springs Train,' and acquired both a name and a long-lasting identity: It was called *The Ghan*, a typically bush Australian shortening of the nick-name *The Afghan Express*. Just how it came about is a subject good for argument in any railway pub, but it's likely the name was bestowed more to disparage than to honour the cameleers whose teams the railway replaced.

Camels were brought to Australia and bred in big numbers in South Australia and the Northern Territory. For decades, camels were the carriers in country too tough for horse or bullock teams. To handle these recalcitrant animals, cameleers were imported too from an area that is now Pakistan. But in the local lore of the outback, these strange men in robes and turbans, with strange

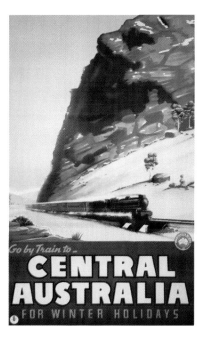

Tourism in Central Australia was pioneered by the railway. The then Commonwealth Railways sent advertising posters Australia wide in the late 1930's, but World War 2 cut short a promising tourist business.

gods, strange ways, strange foods, were believed to come from the mysterious Afghanistan.

They were, therefore, Afghans, 'Ghans, and when one of them was the sole passenger leaving a train at Oodnadatta, a local wit dubbed the train *The Afghan's Express*. Shortened to The Ghan, the name became as much an outback tradition as the train itself. When Australian National Railways built a new track to Alice Springs and planned a prestigious passenger train service from Adelaide to Central Australia there was really no other choice for a name, for even if it had been called something else officially the new name would certainly have been ignored. The Ghan had made its own history, its own legends. It was part of life outback.

The weekly round trip was a travel adventure. The time-table was a matter more of hope than of fact, and often when the elements conspired against the train not only was the hour of arrival indefinite, but even the day and sometimes the week. It once reached Alice Springs six weeks late, when freak floods washed away track and bridges. On another trip it sat on the bank of a flooded river for two weeks. Fresh food ran out, and the driver shot wild goats to feed his passengers.

This was hostile country for man and machine alike. Dry country, with almost no permanent surface water, yet laced with stream beds capable within hours of rising in destructive flood. Heat buckled the steel rails. Termites ate the timber sleepers. Chemicals in the underground water rotted the boilers of steam engines, and the coal they burned had to be brought from far away mines on the east coast.

The old railway which ended at Alice Springs was planned as a north-south Transcontinental line, Adelaide to Darwin. Until 1910, the now Northern Territory was part of South Australia, and the agreement that the Federal Government take it over included the promise that the line the South Australians had built as far north as Oodnadatta would be extended, via Alice Springs, to Darwin. The tracks reached Alice Springs in 1929, but the South Australian negotiators seem to have overlooked the fact that their agreement with the Commonwealth Government contained no time clause, and while the promise has never been revoked, the line to Darwin has never been built. There are inquiries and investigations from time to time into the Alice Springs to Darwin railway. Supporters claim massive potential savings in time and freight costs if ships were able to unload in Darwin and their cargoes railed to the southern cities. Opponents say the line could not pay its way. The north-south line remains a political promise: Neither kept nor formally broken.

The Australian Coat of Arms, cast in metal, was carried on the locomotives of the Commonwealth Railways.

Reflections of Adelaide

Adelaide

Adelaide, the starting point of The Ghan's journey to Central Australia, owes its shape and style to the British Army, in particular to a British Army Surveyor assigned in colonial times to design the future capital city of the free colony, South Australia.

Old and new combines in Adelaide city

Colonel William Light did his work so well that the design he prepared a century and a half ago has remained the blueprint for modern Adelaide, a city now of some one million people who claim it to be one of the world's most successful cities. Its business heart is separated from its suburbs by generous parklands on all four sides, and nowhere in Adelaide is very far from anywhere else. The sportsgrounds are the envy of cities everywhere. The beaches and the bush are close by. In the hills edging the coastal plain micro climates create an environment more European than Australian. Some of the world's best vineyards are half an hour's drive from the city, and again the European heritage is apparent in ordered vineyards and elegant old stone buildings that date from the German settlers who gave to South Australia, in return for refuge from religious persecution in Europe, their skills as farmers, vignerons and wine makers.

For more than a hundred years the wines of South Australia's Barossa Valley were a private treasure because past generations of Australians were not much interested in wines. That changed, suddenly and spectacularly half way through the 20th Century, and the wines of the Barossa now are a national treasure.

The first half hour of The Ghan's journey is quite literally through the backyards of Adelaide, beginning at Australian National's headquarters, and The Ghan's home base, the railway terminal at Keswick.

Once just a station on Adelaide's suburban rail system, Keswick is now the hub of Australian National's passenger network whose rails span the continent

The builders plate and number plate from an original Ghan locomotive. The complete locomotive is part of the extensive collection of Adelaide's Port Dock Railway Museum, Port Adelaide.

Departure time: A commonplace event, yet with an excitement of its own. At Keswick Terminal, Adelaide, The Ghan greets its guests. and prepares to keep its promise to take them on one of the great railway journeys of the world.

A new approach to travel: The Ghan aims to make the journey as memorable as a Central Australian holiday itself, and its crews are told their efforts as hosts are all important.

Dreamtime Lounge

from the Indian Ocean coast at Perth to the Pacific coast at Sydney, and from Adelaide to Central Australia. Keswick is more than a train station: It's a centre of tourist adventure, and the journeys that begin here are listed among the great railway journeys of the world: Adelaide to Sydney, Adelaide to Perth across the vast treeless plain called The Nullarbor, and Adelaide to Alice Springs, Central Australia, the route of The Ghan.

At Keswick The Ghan is prepared for its 48-hour round trip to Alice Springs. The train is washed, the grime of a working railway hosed and scrubbed away by something like a giant car wash.

The pantry is replenished, the bars restocked, cabins cleaned, beds made. The Ghan, and its companion train the Indian Pacific, are new frontiers in Australian railways. They are hotels on the move, rolling resorts, travelling holidays. They mark the change in rail transport from necessity to luxury.

Few people travel by The Ghan just to reach Alice Springs or Adelaide. The Ghan is only partly a transport service. Its passengers are mainly on holiday, and the journey is part of the holiday.

That's the trade The Ghan has captured. Much of Australian National's staff training effort has been to explain to train crews that while they're still very much railway people, they're also in the tourist trade. Their train is an hotel. They're hosts, as well as crew. The success of The Ghan

The Prince of Wales car, built by Commonwealth Railways for visiting Royalty, is available now for commoners: Rich commoners, for the one-way fare is $8,000.

Soundproofed and air-conditioned, the cars of todays Ghan offer luxury available not even to past princes.

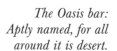

The Oasis bar: Aptly named, for all around it is desert.

Nightfall near Port Augusta. The Flinders Ranges taper down to the sea, and just beyond them, the Australian Outback begins.

Australian National's communications and train control system keeps The Ghan's drivers in radio contact with base.

At a passing loop The Ghan yields the main line to a hurrying east bound Super-Freighter, one of the high-speed, high-tonnage freight trains which link Australia's Pacific and Indian Ocean coasts.

depends more upon them, and the service they offer, than upon whether the train is on time or is late. The railway culture, where the timetable is king and people are its servants, has been turned around: 'To travel hopefully is better than to arrive' has been given a service and commercial edge, while the practicalities of a working railway, the ironclad rules of safety, are never relaxed.

At Australian National's master control centre at Keswick, train controllers prepare a plan for each of The Ghan's journeys, much as aeroplane pilots plan a flight or sea captains a voyage. For The Ghan

Fast container traffic, the railways' money maker, proves the incomparable efficiency of steel wheels on steel rails for longhaul freight transport.

is not alone on its rail-bound voyage across the Australian deserts: It must share tracks with the transcontinental freight railway, the supply trains to the centre, the stock trains from cattle stations of the Territory.

The iron road to the Alice is a single track railway. So trains must take their turn, wait their place, in a traffic pattern which heeds commercial realities. Freight trains, the real money earners, have priority. For unless the freight trains make money, and the railway prospers, the passenger trains might not survive. Although Australian National, alone among Australia's railways, claims to have made

Wheat farming on the Adelaide plains: In the 19th Century this was the granary of Australia.

passenger services pay their way, the real business of railways is freight.

As freight movers the railways are incomparably efficient. One train, one SuperFreighter as they're called on the Transcontinental, is the equivalent of as many as one hundred road trucks. They're three times as fuel efficient as trucks. Their contribution to road safety, and reduced road maintenance, is incalculable.

A few kilometres north of Keswick, The Ghan moves through the Adelaide plains. The South Australian colony was unusual in Australian history because it was set up and developed by free settlers. South Australia had no convict era. It was spared the inhumanity of the convict system which shaped the other Australian colonies.

The farmers, artisans and shopkeepers who came to the early South Australia came voluntarily. It was the dream of cash, not threat of the lash, that motivated them, and the society they formed differed in nature and in outlook from the rest of Australia.

On the plains to the north of Adelaide, the migrant farmers found land that could grow grain as well as anywhere they knew, and for a time, this was the granary of Australia.

The mood of 19th Century South Australia was unbridled optimism, and often lacked reality and common sense. Sites were declared on the Adelaide Plain for a hundred towns and villages. Streets and

Camel teams and man-handled scoops built dams and earth-works on our early railways.

roads were surveyed, and locations selected for twenty new ports along this stretch of coast alone. Few of the towns were ever built, and even fewer ports. The villages that did reach reality, mainly along the route of the first railway, have mostly disappeared in recent times, though some traces remain in the grain silos, white monoliths now rarely used.

The small farmers who opened up this land have mainly gone, their holdings brought together to make bigger farms to meet the economic wisdom of the times.

One remaining monument to the age of optimism is a jetty a kilometre long, the longest, it's said, in the southern hemisphere. It's also a monument to the lack of foresight that so often accompanies official over-optimism, because when a port site was selected here, and named Port Germein, no-one realised the water was too shallow for sailing ships to come anywhere near the coast. So the coast, in the form of a wooden jetty, had to be taken out to the ships.

Port Germein prospered for a while. It was a grain port, its site chosen because it was close to a pass through the Flinders Ranges and a handy shipping point for wheat and wool from the new farming bonanza that was believed to lie beyond the ranges.

But farming failed beyond the Flinders Ranges because officialdom which encouraged settlement, and settlers who responded, mis-read the message of nature. It's happened often in Australia. It probably still happens, when people fail to realise that in much of this huge island, drought is not an occasional phenomenon but the normal climate.

At its best, in a good season, the land is fertile and generous, as it was in the Flinders Ranges when the first explorers found and reported on it. In those brief times of plenty the land was divided up into farms that held out the promise of wealth.

But when the good seasons, the freak seasons, ended and the normal dry times returned, that same land brought the reality of deprivation.

It was more than a failure of farming, because the land itself had been mis-read and permanently damaged. The soil, thin and fragile, couldn't stand the European farming methods which were all the settlers knew. Cultivation fractured the soil into powder, to be blown away as dust or washed away as mud in the rare but savage rain storms. Accustomed over millennia to the soft padded paws of kangaroos and wallabies, it was compressed and ruined by the hard cloven hooves of sheep and cattle. Crops failed, the desert advanced. The settlers left, and the sailing ships came no more to the proud jetty at Port Germein, the biggest in the southern hemisphere.

The ruins of a stone farmhouse stand as a monument to failed farming near the original Ghan railway in the Flinders Ranges, South Australia.

Port Augusta

One port that survived, diversified and prospered became the city of Port Augusta, a transport cross-roads that managed the transition from horse and camel teams and sailing ships to the railway of today.

Spencer Gulf at Port Augusta, the last sight of water until Perth on the Trans Australia Railway.

Like Port Germein, Port Augusta was close to a pass through the Flinders Ranges, the pass called Pichi Richi. Aboriginal tribes used the pass for thousands of years. Camel, horse and bullock teams used it and when the railway age came in the last quarter of the 19th century, Pichi Richi became the iron road to the inland, and part of the route of the original Ghan.

Today, a section of that old railway is preserved as a working museum and people from around the world visit to relish the sight and sound of steam trains on the edge of outback Australia.

Once, Port Augusta drew the ships of the world to safe moorings and deep water wharves at the head of a gulf so deeply carved into the coastline that the

The railway workshops at Port Augusta work to world standards to keep the Australian National fleet rolling.

normal flushing effect of tides is minimised and the water is extraordinarily salty. So much so, that sailors believed they couldn't drown if they fell in, drunk, from their ships at a Port Augusta anchorage. Old graves in the town cemetery prove they were wrong.

The Ghan, southbound, skirts the very tip of Spencer Gulf and approaches Port Augusta.

The great grain races from Australia to Europe, when the clipper ships fought for the glory of the fastest passage home with the first of the new season's wheat, often began from Port Augusta. The windjammers, loaded at great speed from the stacks of bagged wheat on Port Augusta's wharves, would sail south to

its importance as a port was in decline, Port Augusta had grasped a new asset, the railway. As a railway to Darwin had been held out to South Australia as an inducement to yield control of the Northern Territory to the Commonwealth, a railway to Perth was offered as a reward for the colony of Western Aus-

The railway west follows for some distance the narrow coastal plain between the Flinders Ranges and Spencer Gulf. An Australian National freighter, westbound, clears Augusta yard and heads for Central Australia.

the mouth of Spencer Gulf, and south again to the latitude 40 degrees south, then ride before the winds, the Roaring Forties, around the bottom of the world to the South Atlantic, across the Equator and home to England.

The last of the clipper ships came to Port Augusta in the year the second world war began. By the time

tralia to join the new Federation of states of Australia. This promise was kept, and after 12 years of talking work on the east-west transcontinental railway began. It was Australia's first national project, and after all those years of talking, it took only five years to build. Port Augusta, the eastern end of the line, became the railway's headquarters and principal supply point. Vast workshops were built to construct and maintain vehicles and Port Augusta began a new life as a railway town.

Port Augusta is proud of its identity as the city on the edge of the Outback, that vast area of Australia that lacks boundaries and few can say where it begins

There's little more to say about Glendambo!

and ends. Port Augusta holds the outback begins on the western edge of town, but in truth a better boundary is half an hour's train trip further west, a line on the map called the 32nd parallel of latitude. When the railway crosses the 32nd it truly enters outback Australia.

West of Port Augusta, the saltbush ends, the hardy plant which drinks in the sparse moisture of the night air and grows and feeds sheep where no other plant can survive. Where the saltbush ends, the sheep

country ends, and west from here there's little commercial livestock.

There is life though in the busy, dangerous natural world just outside the train window. Most Australian wildlife is nocturnal, and in the cool of the desert night it seeks the food and moisture it must have to survive tomorrow's heat.

Station homestead at Bulgannia near Tarcoola

There is an endless struggle for survival out there in the apparently empty desert, for almost everything that moves is sought as food by something else. For countless time, the balance was kept between eater and eaten, but only in the last hundred years imported animals have so distorted the natural world that it will never recover. The newcomers are the rabbit, the fox and the dreadful feral cat.

Naturalists researching this arid zone are aghast at the environmental damage these pests cause. No native creature in the Australian desert or bush was equipped by nature with defense against predators like cats and foxes. Whole species are under threat, some may already have been wiped out.

Donkeys are one of the many domestic animal species running wild in the outback: Damaging the fragile environment, but far less destructive than the feral cat.

Cats probably came with the railway builders as camp pets. Their offspring, unwanted and abandoned, were left to run wild as construction camps moved on and the process which evolutionists call survival of the fittest brought a very tough breed of cat indeed, murderous to wildlife.

The rabbit poses a different threat: It eats only vegetation, but it eats so thoroughly that the vegetation is demolished rather than eaten down, and a few generations of rabbits can strip land bare of anything that grows. Native grazing animals, kangaroos, wallabies and a myriad of smaller

creatures find nothing is left for them when the rabbits arrive.

The human population of the arid zone is sparse, but of extraordinary variety: Stockmen and station hands on the vast cattle runs, railway people, prospectors, geologists, drilling teams and scientists. The area had a role in the years of the Cold War, when the American military set up at Narrungar, near the railway siding at Pimba, a control and monitoring station for spy-in-the-sky satellites, part of the United States' early warning system against long range ballistic missiles.

Building a Legend

It was a brave decision to build the transcontinental railway, and it's likely that until the work was well under way, no-one realised how difficult it would be. Because nature offered no help whatever: No water, no reliable surface water, along the entire length of the railway. No trees, therefore no timber for structures and sleepers. No fuel for locomotives.

Welded rail on concrete sleepers, Australian National's definition of the Permanent Way.

To begin, teams of surveyors set out simultaneously from Port Augusta and Kalgoorlie, the western terminal. Their camel teams dragged chains across the empty land to mark the path the railway would follow, and when the teams met somewhere in the middle, they realised they'd drawn the line for the longest stretch of straight track in the railway world: Just under 300 miles in the measure of the times, 478 kilometres without a quiver or a curve.

The original Ghan line and the Trans Australia alike, were anything but permanent: Flood and fire, desert heat and termites, made maintenance a constant and costly necessity.

Camel Train, Trans Australia Railway, c. 1912

It's hard for a passenger riding today's Ghan on the section of the transcontinental line from Port Augusta to the junction at Tarcoola, to realise just how harsh the land is on the other side of the train's double glazed windows, how hot it is outside the air conditioning, how desperately dry. With chilled water in the cabins, and ice in the bars, can this be the same world that faced the railway pioneers beginning their push into the desert in 1912?

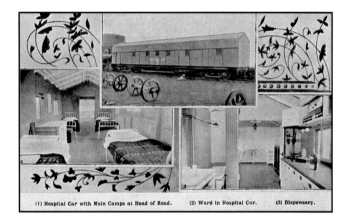

(1) Hospital Car with Main Camps at Head of Road.   (2) Ward in Hospital Car.   (3) Dispensary.

Every drink, every wash, every shave, every baby's bath and animal's water had to be carried in, along with every scrap of food and stick of timber. Work gangs assembled at Port Augusta and Kalgoorlie, and rolling townships were devised to carry men and materials to the worksites. Beyond the rails, camels were both power and transport, and the railway used hundreds of them. They carried surveyors and engineers on exploratory forays ahead of the track-layers; camels carried in the wooden sleepers, hauled

water carts and brought in drinking water in ships tanks strapped to their backs.

Their work done, the camels were let run wild, and their descendants live still in the northern territory. They're said to be the purest strain of camels to be found anywhere in the world and some have been rounded up and exported to the Middle East.

Maintenance gang, Trans Australia Railway

Labor for the line north of Marree was recruited from European refugees who'd fled from the First World War. They suffered dreadfully in the harsh conditions of the Australian outback, quite unprepared for the hard work they had to do and for a climate which transformed the gentle sun of Europe into the daily furnace on the edge of the Simpson Desert.

The old enmities and rivalries of Europe sometimes surfaced in the construction camps. There were fights, and serious injuries, but little of this appears in the official records, where the results of brawls are often described as 'accidents at work.'

A second wave of European immigrants following the Second World War provided labor for track re-building in the 1940s and early 50s. As a condition of entry to Australia, migrants had little choice but to go where the Government directed and do whatever work they were told.

The Iron Man at Impadna, a sculpture designed and built by railway workers, commemorates the laying of the one millionth concrete sleeper on the new Ghan line.

When the decision was made to build the new Ghan line to Alice Springs via Tarcoola, an experienced workforce was found in an unlikely place, the Islands of Torres Strait, between Australia and Papua New Guinea.

It's hard to imagine a greater contrast to the sea-going island life of Torres Strait than the railway construction camps in the outback, yet these islanders had become the railway builders of Australia. They were first recruited to work on the reconstruction of the railway between Mount Isa, in western Queensland, and the port of Townsville, the refining and shipping point for the metals from Mount Isa's mines.

From there, the Torres Strait Islanders moved to railway building projects in the north-west of Western Australia, where vast deposits of iron ore were discovered and linked by rail to new ports. By now more experienced than any other group in Australia, and conditioned to the hard work and tough life of the railways, men whose traditions were in fishing and pearling built the new line to Central Australia.

Freighter to the Alice: At Hesso, 54 km north of Pt. Augusta, an AN freight train to Central Australia has crossed the 32nd parallel, the 'Boundary of the Outback', and heads north-west into the night.

Woomera

Military interest in outback Australia began in the 1940s when the British set up a rocket testing range at Woomera. Britain's cities a few years before had been the first to experience rocket attacks when the Germans launched their V-2 missiles. Now the British wanted their own rockets, and Australia agreed to test shots over the South Australian desert.

The site was chosen for its isolation and its climate. It was famously dry, there were clear skies almost year round, and to the north-west there were 2,000 kilometres of land which became the rocket range. The site was named Woomera, the Aboriginal word for a throwing stick, a kind of lever the Aborigines used to increase the speed and range of a spear throw. Another benefit of the remote desert location was its distance from the eyes of British tax-payers who funded the astronomical cost of eight hundred test firings of rockets and missiles that never quite did what they were supposed to do, until in the 1970s the project, and the rocket range, died.

Woomera has probably the best defended tennis court in the world.

The missile park in Woomera town centre – maintained by the Lions Club, it is somehow a bit disappointing: You drop 20 cents into the slot and nothing happens. The British Government dropped millions of pounds into this place with similar results.

A salt pan near Woomera, named with optimism L a k e Hart.
From the shore opposite, missiles were test fired down the Woomera rocket range.

𝒯 arcoola

Between Port Augusta and Kalgoorlie, along the whole length of one of the world's longest railways, there is only one major junction. The place is Tarcoola, where The Ghan leaves the transcontinental line and turns north towards Central Australia.

Tarcoola was a goldfield, named after a race-horse, a thoroughly Australian approach to things. Gold was found in 1893, the year the horse Tarcoola won the Melbourne Cup. The gold rush was brief, but the railway brought an extension of life. It needed Tarcoola as a service point for steam engines, but the diesels ended that. The construction of the new

Tarcoola Railway Station.

railway to Alice Springs in the 1970s, and the selection of Tarcoola as the junction, gave it yet another reprieve, and the little town on the edge of nowhere can still boast the last pub until Kalgoorlie or the Alice, and a history as a watering place for man and machine.

Tarcoola, the survivor on the edge of the outback, is the exception to the story of so many railway villages in Australia. Created by the railways, then abandoned by railway progress, their sites lie unmarked along the railway maps of the nation. Sometimes a building remains, or a stockyard, or a rusting loop line on rotting sleepers, left in place because that was cheaper than to remove it.

One railway, one road, and inevitably they'll cross paths: Ferguson, 377 km north of Pt. Augusta

Gold mine, Tarcoola. Miners in the last century felled the trees that once stood here to provide fuel for their machinery and their camps. Today, some of the mines of Tarcoola are working again, using the carbo-cyanide method to extract gold from the debris of past mining.

TARCOOLA – THE RACE-COURSE

Rolly St.Clair, 1980

I'll take you to the race-course that is neither flash nor grand,
It hasn't any fancy turf, nor even any stand.
It's far cry from being a Flemington or Randwick or the rest,
But you've never seen a course to match Tarcoola's out Nor'west.

It's a dinkum Aussie course without pretence and vain display;
With stewards, judges and the like, it's honest as the day.
No Phar Laps, Tullochs grace this course, no winners of
world fame,
But swabs are never needed in Tarcoola's racing game.

It isn't Bernborough romping home, and the jockey's not George
Moore,
But the crowd cheers every winner with a full-throated roar;
And our decent, hardy station lads who ride the hardy mounts,
Take this pleasure from the contest, for the winning's not what
counts.

It's a dinkum Aussie race-course of the battlers out Nor'West,
Of dinkum folk and honest hearts who make their fun with zest.
No, you haven't enjoyed a meeting if you've not been out Nor'West,
On the old Tarcoola race-course, where the sport is at it's best.

Rolly St.Clair lives in Tarcoola. He's an old railway hand who worked on the Ghan line for some 20 years, and here shows a piece from its history: A section of rail bearing the brand 'Goverment Gums', the original name of the township of Farina.

Tarcoola Pub: The last pub until Kalgoorlie or The Alice

Coober Pedy

When white men began to dig for opals on the eastern edge of the Great Victoria Desert, they found their shafts and drives were more comfortable places to be than their surface tents and shacks which baked all day in fierce sun and froze all night in desert cold.

So the miners made their homes underground, and the Aborigines of the region, who'd never seen anything like it, were much amused. In their experience only animals lived

Coober Pedy opals for sale to the world

in holes in the ground. They described this extraordinary behaviour by white men in words that sounded like 'Coober Pedy,' and that's the name now of the richest opal field in the world. Coober Pedy means something like 'cave men,' or 'people living in burrows.' It's about eighty kilometres east of the railway line. And there, people have created – not built, but excavated – an underground township.

Miners and their families have made neither primitive dugouts nor caves, but homes as comfortable and well fitted out as any surface house anywhere. They enjoy a year round temperature which ignores the extremes of the Great Victoria Desert a few metres above their heads. And from their nearby diggings, they mine one of the world's most sought-after gem stones.

How much they mine no-one knows, or is prepared to tell: Three quarters of the world's top quality opal production comes from this Coober Pedy field, one figure suggests. But the true statistics of Austral-

Sunday morning, Coober Pedy. Church goers' cars park on in front of the underground church.

ia's opal production may never be known. Such authorities as Tax Departments would very much like to find out, but opal mining is one of the last truly

Miners cottage, Mintabie, built from rock which once hid the precious opal.

individual activities left in Australia, and it keeps its business very much to itself. Opal miners are very private people. Theirs is a very private industry, whose secrets are buried as deep as the gems it seeks. Deep buried also, according to folk lore, are some of those who sought its secrets.

To geologists, opal is a quartz like form of hydrated silica. To gemologists, jew-

Water is scarce in Coober Pedy. At the coin operated roadside water dispenser 20 cents buys 30 litres.

ellers and buyers around the world, it's a magical stone with the ability to manipulate light so that colors of infinite variety and intensity appear to be generated inside the polished gem.

There are other opal fields in Australia: Among them Andamooka, Mintabie, White Cliffs and Lightning Ridge. But it's Coober Pedy, 80 kilometres east of The Ghan's railway, where people live in holes in the ground, that the world sees as the symbol of Australian opal and pays the price the glorious gem stone commands.

The Oodnadatta Track, one of the legendary roads of the outback, starts at Marla, which also is the access point to Mintabie. Beyond lie the lands of the Pitjantjatjara people, and travellers there need a permit to proceed.

↘ Next two pages
The understated eloquence of the signs of Coober Pedy.

A Miner's Story
by Margaret Mackay

Elizabeth Maria Guba arrived in Coober Pedy with her husband Bernd and two young children on June 6, 1975. The young family had been living in the Sydney suburb Manly since their arrival from Germany in 1970.

Through friends they had become interested in opal and on some of their holidays visited Lightning Ridge in a group. During one such holiday, the friends gathered enough opal from 'gouging' that they were able to divide the spoils into dinner plate size lots.

In 1975 another couple, also interested in opal, discussed with the Gubas a mining partnership at Coober Pedy. The group was made up of four men, Elizabeth and the two children. Three of the four men pooled their resources to purchase the mining equipment. The Gubas had set out with $9,000. However, like a lot of well intended beginings, the partnership broke up after only two months, and the Gubas found themselves left with $120 cash, a caravan, a light truck and the York hoist.

The couple reassessed their position but realised that their son was settled in school and their daughter was about to start kindergarten. They agreed on a short term plan – to work as hard as possible mining and surviving and, if in the time things had not progressed, they would return to Sydney.

Raw opal, awaiting skilled cutting and polishing to reveal its flashing beauty.

It was at this point that Elizabeth began mining. 'A lot of wives did mine with their husbands then', recalls Elizabeth, and remembers that she thoroughly enjoyed it, as did most of the women. 'It wasn't just the excitement of finding opal, because that hope was always there, but the work was interesting and adventurous. Sometimes occupying the children was awkward while we worked,' she said, 'so we couldn't always put in the hours we wanted to. To overcome this we took the children down into the mine to play about whilst we worked and used jack-hammering instead of blasting to make it safer. Whilst working above the ground, for a few months we restrained them in safety harnesses until they got used to the dangers of shafts, then all was well.'

Elizabeth would not have chosen mining as a career, and thinks she can speak for most of the women in Coober Pedy. Women usually would not mine alone, finding it difficult to succeed. However, in a partnership, the women worked just as hard as they were able to, as did the men. Women generally did not feel as though mining was an equal opportunity occupation. A female partner was viewed more as a helper, although some women did operate with a man in a totally equal partnership.

Open cut opal mine, Mintabie.

For a while the couple lived in Bulls Caravan Park where Elizabeth was able to work as a cleaner. This helped to pay rental costs while the mining got going. She also did cleaning at the town amusement centre. Later she helped out at the Umooma mine, selling opal and translating for the bus-loads of German tourists.

In 1978 the young family moved into their own dugout in German Gully. They had achieved considerable success in opal mining and now enjoyed more efficient mining equipment. All this appeared as symbols of success, but Elizabeth felt it was reward for all their hard work. 'We came from nothing basically', she recalls, 'but $120 and virtually our bare hands.'

Finke River

A measure of the vast dryness of inland Australia is the fact that along the whole journey of 1,555 kilometres from Adelaide to Alice Springs, The Ghan crosses only two major watercourses. They appear on maps as the Rivers Hugh and Finke but for most of the time they are rivers of sand, with hardy River Red Gums driving their roots deep into the river beds in search of moisture deep underground.

Substantial bridges cross both stream beds because both can become dangerously flooded if there's heavy rain upstream. In the days of the original Ghan line to Alice Springs, the Finke had an appetite for rail bridges: Six months after the rails reached the Alice in 1929, the Finke came down in flood and washed

Now: Finke River Bridge, Mk III:
Hopefully flood proof, but as yet untried by freak flood.

away the new bridge north of Oodnadatta. No trains ran for six weeks, while a stone causeway was laid, and that served until the early 1960s when a new bridge was built. It too was destroyed by the flooded Finke in 1967. The Finke bridge on the standard gauge route of The Ghan is as flood proof as can be built. The Finke has not yet tested its strength.

The Finke River is believed by some authorities to be one of the oldest watercourses on earth, following the same path today as it has since pre-history, when this modern desert was a vast rain forest. The country still comes to spectacular life occasionally, when nature chooses just to add water.

The Northern Territory has 2,800 plant types, many of them existing in a kind of hibernation and ready to explode in new growth whenever enough

Then: A flood has washed the rails away, and the old Ghan is due for one of its once infamous delays.

The monolith called 'Chambers' Pillar'
close to Finke River bridge.

rain falls. The bare red country is then briefly green. The dusty leaves of eucalypts, the gum trees, have new life and sparkle. Streams run, waterholes fill. There are huge and immediate migrations of birds. 350 species live in the Northern Territory, from Wedge-tailed eagles two metres across the wings to tiny parrots. Budgerigars, bred and caged worldwide as household pets, fly free in the Territory. The water draws the mammals, more than a hundred species are found here. The human pre-history of the Northern Territory is inexact: It was perhaps 50,000 to 60,000 years ago that people first came on bamboo rafts from the islands of Asia, and they were the ancestors of the present Aborigines. Some 30,000 years ago the first human traces were left in Central Australia. The centre then was green and well-watered, but Aboriginal habitation continued through thousands of years of increasing aridity.

Aborigines knew the great sandstone monolith as Uluru. White explorers called it Ayers Rock. Now back under Aboriginal control, its name is again Uluru.

The Aborigines were hunters and gatherers rather than farmers, but they did make use of one farming tool, fire. To modern farming bushfires are immensely damaging, but to the Aborigines fire was tractor and plough, seed and fertiliser, the agent of renewal that brought new growth and young animals, and timed the year round food supply.

There are persuasive arguments that the Aborigines in fact managed the fragile soils of Central Australia far better than the Europeans who pushed them off their land to clear the way for cattle, thus beginning a process of soil degradation which in some areas is beyond economic repair.

With the white man came the notion of land ownership, either by individuals, the Cattle Kings some were called, or by Government. The Aboriginal people had no concept of ownership of land: Rather, they were owned by the land, and the land was generous to them. At the time of the first European exploration of inland Australia, the Aborigines had a standard of living far ahead of the mass populations of the old world. They had a wider variety of food, fresher and of better quality than the people of the industrial cities of Britain and Europe could imagine.

The land, the core of Aboriginal life and culture, was for the newcomers a commodity to be bought and sold or gained by Government grant. It was a

A tribute to the rock and a test of physical strength: Tourists climb to the top of Uluru.

Two such opposed cultures could not co-exist, and it was the Aborigines, inevitably, who lost. For more than a hundred years they were treated as intruders and nuisances. Their social, tribal structures were threatened and in some places broke down. An old and intricate fabric of laws, customs and traditions quickly unravelled. White missionaries came, with the best of intentions, but they too pressured the Aborigines to put aside the beliefs of millenia and take up the same principles white men claimed to observe.

source of wealth, a measure of prosperity. Land was there to be developed: An argument of the times held that the Aborigines had no claim to the land because they had done nothing to develop it.

The Aborigines were confused, because while some whites demanded their conversion to the new ways, other whites who claimed the same beliefs were stealing land and mounting murderous attacks on Aborigines who resisted.

It took more than a hundred years for attitudes to change. A turn for the better began in 1967 when a majority of Australians voted to give the national Government control of Aboriginal issues. To Australia's shame, it was only then that Aborigines were acknowledged as Australian citizens.

In the Northern Territory pioneering land rights laws for Aborigines were introduced in 1976, and by the 90's about a quarter of all the land in the Territory was under Aboriginal control, open to visitors only by permit.

A thousand years, perhaps ten thousand years ago, Northern Territory ochre pits provided materials for Aboriginal artists.

Hermannsburg Mission, founded by Lutherans, incurred official displeasure when it gave shelter to Aboriginal offenders against white mens law.

You see the smoke at Kapunda.
The steam puffs regularly.
Showing quickly, it looks like frost.
It runs like running water.
It blows like a spouting whale.

(from G.Taplin: The Narringeri, 1873)

Aborigines and the Ghan Train

by Dick Kimber

When the Kaurna people of the Adelaide plains and coastal country first saw a train they were interested, excited, fearful. No doubt they, as with their neighbours, composed a song in which, as might be expected of people who gained much of their livelihood from the sea, they likened the puffing steam train to a spouting whale.

The railways gradually extended north-westerly to Port Augusta, always following a decade or two behind earliest European exploration and settlement. As a consequence, all Aborigines within any proximity to the route followed had always had considerable previous contact with the colonists. By 1879–1890, at which period the railway was extended north from Port Augusta to Oodnadatta, most Nukunu, Pangkala, Kujani and Arabunna people – the traditional owners of the lands north of Port Augusta – were no longer frightened by the arrival of trains. It was only the more remote people, migrating in to the line for the first time, who were terrified. From a safe distance they saw people inside the speeding train,

*The local law in Finke:
Little room for legal argument.*

and understandably translated what they saw in their own world view. Here was a giant devil-snake which had swallowed many people. The poor unfortunate people were trying to escape!

Each railway station and siding became a place to which cattle could be walked from distant cattle stations by drovers, many of whom were Aboriginal stockmen. They, as much as the drovers of European origin, became legendary-heroic figures, and Douglas Stewart captured the romantic image of such a drover on his way down the Birdsville Track to the major rail town, Marree.

SOMBRERO

In a cowboy hat and a dark-green shirt,
Lithe on a piebald pony,
The blackfellow rode through the coolabah-trees
Where the creek was dry and stony.

Here's fifty horses from Pandie Pandie
To drove to far Marree
But before I start on the track again
I'll boil up a billy of tea.

Oh he was as dark as the gibber stones
And took things just as easy
And a white smile danced on his purple lips
Like an everlasting daisy.

The horses strayed on the saltbush plain
And he went galloping after,
The green shirt flew through the coolabah-trees
Like budgerigars to water.

And then what need had he to sigh
For old men under the gibbers
When he was free as the winds that blow
Along the old dry rivers?

He had the lubras' hot wild eyes,
His green shirt and sombrero,
He rode the plains on a piebald horse
And he was his own hero.

The towns became centres which attracted local area Aborigines for a variety of reasons. Ration depots were established to assist the old and infirm, active young men obtained jobs with camel teams taking the loading (stores and other goods) from the rail towns to remote localities, other men became police trackers, women received training as domestic servants, and so on. There was undoubtedly prejudice, exploitation, and racism, yet relationships could be friendly and mutually helpful. The owners of strings of camels, for instance, allowed Aborigines the use of camels for travel to important sites and to attend ceremonies.

A Depression in South Australia in the early 1890's meant that the railhead remained at Oodnadatta for decades. However in 1929 it finally reached Alice Springs, in the land of the Aranda people. By this time motor vehicle and aeroplane had been invented and tourism was on the increase. Although the world-wide Great Depression of 1929–1933, then World War 2, greatly curbed tourist travel on 'the Ghan', by the late 1940's it began to increase again. Aborigines were invariably a focal point of interest at any stop, with tourists often insensitive in their desire for photographs.

Now, although relatively few do, Aborigines may work on 'the Ghan', travel on it, or even take photographs of tourists.

Finke Siding lives on, a township now, the centre of an Aboriginal settlement. The railway station remains, a building without its tracks. The connection to the world outside, the reason for its existence, has gone with the scrappers.

At Heavitree Gap, near Alice Springs, The Ghan passes a natural sculpture of the history of the earth, a diagram of the origins of the MacDonnell Rnges.

Alice Springs

The Ghan enters Alice Springs through a pass in the MacDonnell Ranges called Heavitree Gap. It's a place of geological wonder, where nature has sliced open the old rock to reveal in cross section how the upthrusts of rock formed the Ranges. The Gap was a place of power and magic to Aborigines. Young tribesmen could go there only in the company of an elder. Women were not allowed there at all, but made to walk over the range. White men had little concern for the sacred sites of the Aborigines. They saw only a handy pass through the range, and they built there first the road, then the railway.

The first white to explore Central Australia was Charles Sturt. In 1844 he set out from Adelaide to search for mythical inland sea whose existence was an article of faith in the early colonies. He reached the eastern edge of the Simpson Desert but illness and lack of water turned his expedition back. The explorer John McDouall Stuart succeeded in 1862 where Sturt had failed. Stuart was surveying a route for the proposed overland telegraph line, which was later built along his survey line and completed as far as Darwin in 1872. The telegraph put Australia in touch with the world, and was directly responsible for the creation of the city of Central Australia, Alice Springs.

The spring, an oasis in the dry centre, was an obvious site for a telegraph repeater station. Its original name was Alice's Spring, named for the wife of the overland telegraph builder, Charles Todd. The town which developed nearby was called Stuart, and when the railway came in 1929, its terminus was still called Stuart.

Alice Springs, the city of Central Australia

Technology versus the elements in Alice Springs: Day becomes as night and freight handling is tough going when a dust storm brings the desert to town.

But people preferred the name Alice Springs. The writer Neville Shute set a popular novel there, *A Town Called Alice*, and the book and the later film helped the Alice become Australia's most famous inland town.

The Todd River parallels the railway through Heavitree Gap. It's another of those Central Australian rivers of sand which are capable of sudden floods. Once a year, at the height of the dry season, the Todd is the site of a regatta, known with outback irony as Henley-on-Todd. The 'boats' are bottomless structures, and their crews, torsos out the top and legs out the bottom, propel them at a smart trot along the sandy river bed.

A mural at Alice Springs shopping centre traces the history of transport in Central Australia.

At MacDonnell siding, just south of Alice Springs, an operating museum preserves steam locomotives and rolling stock.

Alice Springs City centre

Builder's plate from an early Diesel locomotive on the old Ghan line.

While Alice Springs owes its origins to the overland telegraph line, its modern prosperity stems from the arrival of the railway, the original Ghan line, in 1929. As settlement of the Northern Territory expanded, its vast cattle stations established, its mineral wealth revealed, Alice Springs, the railhead, was the natural transport focus of the emerging economy. The city of Alice Springs in the 1990s is

The Todd River bisects Alice Springs.
They'll jump it, but in flood times it's deep and wide.

Palm valley

a small, complex community of some 28,000 permanent residents plus a seasonal or floating population of 4,000. Its industries range from transport and distribution to servicing two of Australia's major gold-fields, and in a secret establishment named Pine Gap, a few kilometres out of town, the Americans maintain a facility whose business is a kind of international espionage. Australian defence observers believe Pine Gap's business is the control and monitoring of a system of spy satellites which intercept radar and electronic communications in areas of the globe in which the Americans are interested.

Pine Gap adds about 2,500 people to the population of Alice Springs, and the American influence, though deliberately low-key, has brought baseball and gridiron football to central Australia. Tourism has made Alice Springs an international city. Its tourist trade approaches half a million visitors a year, and the service industry which has developed on the base of tourism is now big business. Tourism, mining, oil and natural gas production and cattle grazing are the economic strengths of the Alice Springs region. Alice Springs is the access point to some of Australia's natural wonders: Uluru, the red arkose sandstone

In Kings Canyon

monolith; The Olgas, a group of 36 vast rocks scattered as though by the hand of a giant; Palm Valley, a haunting relic of times long past when Central Australia was well watered and lush; and the ancient Aboriginal rock engravings of N'Dhala Gorge.

A lonely flagpole marks the Lambert Centre between Alice Springs and Finke. Set up by a group of 4WD-enthusiasts it marks the geographical centre of Australia.

Serpentine Gorge

ROLAND ROBINSON

I AM AT DEEP WELL

I am at Deep Well where the spirit-trees
writhe in cool white limbs and budgerigar-
green hair along the watercourse carved out
in deep red earth, a red dry course that goes
past the deep well, past the ruined stone
homestead where the wandering blacks make camp
(their campfire burning like a star at rest
among dark ruins of the fallen stone)
to find the spinifex and ochre-red
sandhills of a land inhabited by those
tall dark tribesmen with long hair, and voices
thin and far and, deepening, like a sea.
I am at Deep Well where the fettlers' car
travels towards the cool blue rising wave,
that is the Ooraminna Range, and starts
those pure birds screaming from the scrub to swerve,
reveal their pristine blush in wings and breasts,
to scatter, settle and flower the desert oak.
Here I have chosen to be a fettler, work
to lay the red-gum sleepers, line and spike
the rails with adze and hammer, shovel and bar,
to straighten up and find my mates, myself
lost in the spinifex flowing down in waves
to meet the shadow-sharpened range, and know
myself grown lean and hard again with toil.
Here, in the valley camp where hills increase
in dark blue depths, the desert hakea stands
holding the restless finches and a single star.

The remains of a dead railway, Henry Hill,
between Alice Springs and Finke

One of Australias best known poets, Roland Robinson was born in Ireland. He came to Australia in the age of nine years. At fourteen he was already working on a sheep station in outback NSW. Later in his working life he was a horse-trainer, jockey, fencer, dam builder, factory worker, cleaner, art school model, member of a ballet company, gardener, crocodile and snake catcher, and greenkeeper of a golfcourse. During the Second World War, he objected to military service, and had to work on the Ghan line as a fettler, where *I am at Deep Well* was written. He was the first white poet to collect and translate Aboriginal poetry and prose. He died in 1992.

Cattle loading ramp at Pootnoora railway siding

Old Traces Old Faces

Outback Australia is crossed by a network of roads and paths known as Tracks. Some follow traditional trade routes of Aboriginal tribes, others the paths of original white explorers. Others are newer, connecting station to station, camp to camp.

One of the most colorful in history and route is the Oodnadatta Track. It links the original Ghan line at Oodnadatta with the new track, the new township, Marla, 218 kilometres away. It leads from Oodnadatta south to Marree and eventually to Port Augusta. At Marree, it meets the legendary Birdsville Track to Queensland, skirting the north-eastern edge of the Simpson Desert. The track has carried the feet of Aborigines, the boots of explorers, the hooves of camels, and now the tyres of trucks and cars.

It offers access to what traces remain of the original Ghan railway, and in isolated and now near-abandoned railway settlements live still some of the people whose lives were the old railway.

Thanks to the Oodnadatta Pink Roadhouse many of the Old Ghan relicts are signposted.

Reg Dodd had been a railway man for 26 years. He is now Progress and Projects Officer for the Marree Arabunna Peoples Committee.

Reg Dodd lives at Marree. A railwayman for 26 years, he saw the last Old Ghan through in August 1956, and he's a good man to talk to about the history of the line.

The first narrow-gauge (3'6") train ran from Port Augusta to Quorn in June 1879, Reg Dodd says. The next year the extension to Hawker was opened, then to Beltana. The rails reached a spot first called Gum Waterhole, and later Government Gums in 1882, and to recognise the importance of the place as the railhead until 1884, it was re-named Farina. The

The Oodnadatta track draws tourist explorers of Outback Australia.

railway went on to Marree in 1884 and to the terminus at Oodnadatta in 1891. There were no such luxuries as sleeping cars. They came in the 1920s. Until then, trains to Oodnadatta stopped overnight in Quorn and their passengers slept in hotels. The Federal Government took over the line from South Australia in 1911, promising to extend the tracks as far as Darwin. They got as far as Alice Springs in 1929, just in time for the depression, and that was as far as work ever went.

In 1957 the narrow gauge track was replaced by broad gauge (5'3") as far as Marree, which became a change of gauge station

A 'piggy-back' wagon. Trains of them once carried narrow gauge vehicles over broad gauge tracks, an attempt to overcome the madness of three gauges in one railway system.

with a population of 350, mostly railworkers employed to transfer freight from broad to narrow gauge vehicles. At its peak, Marree handled 50 trains each week.

But delays in trans-shipment meant freight took seven days from Adelaide to Alice Springs. Road trucks took 24 hours, the railway couldn't compete and its days were numbered.

The passenger train ran fortnightly, the freighter in the alternate weeks. Locals named the passenger train the Flash Ghan, a wry comment on its average speed and its sleeping berths and dining car. The goods train they called the Dirty Ghan.

Ambrose Lyons, known along the old Ghan line as 'Aspro', went to work for the railway in 1949. He worked in the Dining Car, based at Quorn. Aspro recalls that passenger trains would leave Port Augusta with sleeper and sitting cars, picking up the Diner and its crew at Quorn for the six-day round trip to Alice Springs. "The one way trip took 44 hours, if there were no floods."

He remembers being stuck on the bank of the Hamilton River north of Oodnadatta for a week. The dining car ran out of food, and supplies had to be dropped from an aeroplane. The Finke presented frequent wet season problems.

"On one trip, we came to the Finke about eight at night. [This was at the time between bridges, when a causeway carried the track over the river bed.] We didn't know it was flooded. Usually, Horsehoe Bend cattle station, out from Rumbelow, upstream, would let the railway know when the flood passed there and we'd have an idea when it'd get to the railway, but this trip no-one knew it was coming down. Well, we hit the Finke, the water was running up to the steps of the cars. We went through, stopped on the other side to dry out the brakes, and steamed on. Steam engines could go through eighteen inches of water but the diesels only three inches because of the electrical gear underneath them.

Bush humor on an abandoned NSU locomotive at Marree.

Then, there were the grasshoppers, plague locusts, which one year were so thick on the track at Oodnadatta that the locomotive's wheels slipped and skidded and a second engine had to push from the back to get the Ghan started.

"There were fettlers' camps every 20 to 30 miles along the track. There were often derailments, the heat would buckle the rail. White ants would eat out the centres of the sleepers, and they'd fall apart. The new line has concrete sleepers, low maintenance, and now there's only two fettlers' camps all the way from Augusta to the Alice.

"Air conditioning on the Old Ghan was when you put the windows up. You'd get hot air and dust. There were fans on the walls, they'd just move the dust around.

The sheets on the bunks would be stained red. No refrigeration, of course, in the dining car, just ice boxes. We'd fill up with ice at Quorn, then re-stock in Alice."

At Curdimurka, The Ghan Preservation Society's small membership has maintained some railway cottages, the water treatment plant and tank and the Stuart Creek Bridge, a lacy structure of 57 wrought iron spans 433 metres long, a bridge to no-where since its western embankment, half a kilometre long, was washed away in a 1989 flood. Every second year, the Society hosts the Curdimurka Outback Ball, a black tie event which draws as many as 2,000 people to the one-time railway village.

Railwayman Ron Davey is the stuff of railway legend, his lifetime on the trains includes time worked on two railway classics, the original Ghan and the

Eric Oldfield was born in Marree. He runs a sheep station and one of the town's two shops.

trans-continental supply train called the 'Tea and Sugar'. Nowadays he's the storeman on the Tea and Sugar, serving out supplies of food and life's necessities for the families in the few remaining railway villages along the trans-continental line.

Ron joined the original Ghan as a dining car waiter, and he rose to the status of conductor while the Old Ghan still ran.

Conductors were a rare breed of men, their duties an inexact blend of railwayman and hotelier. Theirs was the responsibility for their passengers'

safety, comfort, and even entertainment. It was this latter role that Ron Davey best remembers, the practical jokes, the strictly unofficial side to the long hours between The Alice and Adelaide.

Thirty years or so back, he recalls, there was a rabbit plague araound Alice Springs. Train crews would catch a few and smuggle them aboard the southbound Ghan. Travellers opening their cabin doors to go to breakfast would find the corridors alive with bewildered bunnies. And once, once only, someone brought aboard a young kangaroo, a Joey, and let it loose in the sleeping cars.

Ruins of Farina

Everyone aboard the old Ghan was fair game for the crew's jokes, but groups of young women - 'sheilas' in the slang of the time - were in for special attention. One conductor, nameless even so many years later, once went from cabin to cabin while their

The magnet of water draws birds in their thousands to abandoned but still serviceable railway water tanks along the old Ghan line. At Coward Springs the railway's bore feeds the most remote swimming pool in Australia ... and to the outback traveller, the most refreshing.

young occupants were at dinner and sewed up the seleves of any pyjamas he could find. Railway records contain no mention of the scenes that resulted. Understandable really, for The Ghan was the Ghan, and for practically its whole life, the extraordinary happended everyday.

Train crews got to know many of their passengers because in the time of the old Ghan there were few tourists. Most passengers lived along the track, their children went south by train to school. Ambrose Lyons watched some of the cattle station children grow up, and themselves become station managers.

"The Old Ghan had the love of the people who worked it, but it was a love that developed from memory rather than during the experience. That was just hard work, hard, hot, uncomfortable."

'Half past ten' says the camel clock in Marree. Built from railway sleepers, the ingenious sun-dial is a memorial to the 'Ghans and their camels.

A fghan Cameleers

by Christine Stevens

The train that continues to run from Adelaide to Alice Springs, known as the 'Ghan', was originally known, colloquially, as the 'Afghan Express'. It roughly follows the route travelled last century and early this century by strings of pack-camels, as they plied their way through the North of South Australia and into the heart of the continent. These camel-strings were known as 'camel trains', and were attended by handlers from Afghanistan and the North-West of India.

The 'Afghan Express' was regularly met at its northern stations, and its various northward pushing railheads, by camel-trains waiting to either be delivered of their loads, or to receive new lading, their Afghan attendants often fulfilling vital cartage contracts for the developing pastoral and mining industries. Camels were then the most suitable cartage animals working the desert inland of Australia. They were dromedaries, imported from the North-West Frontier Province of British India, and from across the border into Afghanistan. These animals, which originated centuries earlier in Saudi Arabia, were singularly suited to the harsh, hot and dry conditions of the Australian inland, and their handlers, too, adapted well, most having originated from the tribal regions of the harsh landscape of Afghanistan, in contrast to the origins of the predominantly British settlers.

From 1867 until around 1920 perhaps 6000 to 10,000 camels were imported into Australia (no official records have been found), with perhaps two thousand to four thousand Afghan handlers. This was the era of camel cartage in Australia, of the prominence of the camel as the superior means by which the great mass of inland Australia was both explored and opened for pastoral and mineral exploitation. From the 1880's the camel carrying industry was operated almost exclusively by Afghan merchants and Afghan cameleers.

Recognition of the potentiality of the camel in Australia began with the success of the camels that carried the Burke and Wills Exploration Expedition in 1860, in the great crossing of the continent from south to north. A few camels escaped and were spotted by John McKinlay's search party. The party included the pastoralist and philanthropist, Thomas Elder, who afterwards initiated and funded the first importation of camels and Afghan handlers for a commercial carrying enterprise to

The mosque in Marree

service the drought ravaged north-east of South Australia. The enterprise, and its camel breeding stud, operated from one of Elder's pastoral properties, Beltana station, in the Flinders Ranges area for nearly two decades. Commercial camel cartage worked the North of South Australia, between pastoral stations and mining ventures and the earliest railheads, as rail transport gradually progressed northwards from Adelaide.

However, by the early 1880's, when the railhead reached Farina, and soon afterwards, Hergott Springs (today's Marree), the camel carrying industry had become dominated by the Afghans themselves, operating independently from Elder. The brothers, Faiz and Tagh Mahomet, owned a large company based at Hergott Springs (Marree), and in the early 1890's began a branch of their company on the gold fields of Western Australia. Camel cartage proliferated across the inland, servicing pastoral and mining industries and maintaining isolated communities. Camel trains travelled from railheads and port towns of supply to lonely isolated groups, returning to railheads and port towns with the products of inland industry. Along the 'Ghan' train route, the Oodnadatta railhead opened in 1890, and the Alice Springs railhead not until 1929. On the outskirts of each of the railheads, and near the port towns of supply, Afghan settlements developed near camel pasturage. They were known as 'Afghan-towns' or 'Ghantowns'.

Camel trains and Afghan handlers were constantly leaving and returning to their Ghantowns, constantly loading and unloading at the railheads and constantly making the long trips across the deserts. On the station platforms groups of Afghans would also await mail or personal parcels, milling with townspeople and bush characters in the excitement of an expected train. Turbanned men, bearded in baggy trousers and loose tops, sometimes bejewelled and scented, spoke Pushtu and Dari, and perhaps a little English. Their women, generally secluded back at the Ghantown, were mostly Europeans; widows, deserted wives and sometimes ex-prostitutes. They also married Aboriginal women, for the men brought no women from their homeland. There was a temporariness of their contracts, generally for a three year period, but which was often renewed. Many never returned, though some had wives back in Afghanistan and the North-West Provinces of India. As Muslims, it was permitted to take another wife, for the Koran stated a man could have up to four wives.

One incident, on the railway station platform at Hergott Springs (Marree), while a group were awaiting the arrival of the 'Afghan Express', illustrates some of the cultural features of Afghan society early this century in outback Australia.

In 1904, a young cameleer, called Sher Khan, was betrothed to a girl of fourteen years, the daughter of an Afghan camel merchant from the Hergott Springs (Marree) Ghantown and his European wife. The marriage was arranged according to tradition, and a brideprice was negotiated, a substantial amount of which was paid by the young cameleer before he set out on a long delivery trip with a camel train to earn the balance. But a few weeks later a wealthier Afghan made the girl's father a higher offer, and man and girl were hastily married. Word soon reached Sher Khan through the cameleer network, for not only was he robbed and betrayed, but his honour was at stake. Traditional revenge (Puchtunwali) was necessary to restore honour, if not economics and recourse to a wife.

Sher Khan made his way from beyond Birdsville to the Farina railway station and hid on board the 'Afghan Express' to await his moment. As the 'Afghan Express' hissed into the Hergott Springs (Marree) station, to be met by a noisy group of Afghans and others, gunshots suddenly rang out. The Afghan who had usurped Sher Khan to the merchant's daughter fell to the ground with nine bullet wounds in his body. A turbanned figure was seen fleeing from the train. Pursuit was slow in starting, and Sher Khan disappeared, later to be captured and tried for attempted murder.

The usurper survived the shooting, but after his return to the Ghantown, was tormented by rifle shots fired into his house in the dead of night by Sher Khan's supporters.

The Afghans were strict Muslims, adhering to the five pillars of Islam, performing the five prayer sessions each day, even when 'on the road', and keeping the fasts, festivals and taboos. They built bush mosques at the Ghantowns, and from cameleer donations, more substantial mosques in the major supply cities. At the Ghantowns, date palms graced the gardens of the galvanised iron houses, the entrances to mosques, and stood in water channelled rows for production of the 'Prophet's fruit', eaten at the end of each day's fast during Ramadan.

Afghans took curries to bush society, employed Aborigines as camel assistants, indulged in their narcotic 'culture' of marihuana, hashish and opium (but never the forbidden alcohol, so much part of other bush 'culture'), and danced beside open fires to the sounds of Afghan instruments. They buried their dead in areas set aside in the rail-town cemeteries and in their traditional manner of alignment, with the face of the deceased turned towards the Holy City of Mecca.

Noel Fullerton (l) and Billy Swan (r). Noel runs the Virginia Camel Farm 80 km south of Alice Spriings.

The presence of this unique, exotic culture existed for some half a century and more, at inland rail-towns, towns through which the 'Afghan Express', and the later 'Ghan' train travelled. Today, in the 1990's, the only traces of this exceptional piece of Australia's multicultural history are the few remains of Ghantowns, the unique memorials in rail-town and port-town cemeteries, landmarks bearing Afghan names, like Saddadeen's Range (near Alice Springs), Mahomet Street (Alice Springs) and Kamran's Well (near Uluru), the thousands of feral camels that roam the inland of Australia, and, of course, the descendants of these cameleers and their 'Australian' wives. The most important legacy given to the nation by these Afghans and their intrepid beasts is undoubtedly themselves; their vital role in exploration and in the opening of the inland

Allowed to run wild when their work was done, the camels of Central Australia are bred now for export to the Middle East.

of the continent for pastoralism and mining. But the legacy that lives on in prominence and in name form is that of the train know as the 'Ghan'.

Buried in the land they helped build: Afghan graveyard, Marree.

A railway water tower on the Oodnadatta Track, a lonely monument to a unique railway, and to the age of steam.

The Algebuckina bridge 53 km south of Oodnadatta

Preserving the Heritage

The factor of enthusiasm keeps parts of the old line alive and active: The Old Ghan Preservation Society at Alice Downs, a few kilometres south of Alice Springs at the Stuart Highway, maintains a railway museum and operates a line of 26 kilometres length between Mac Donnell and Ewaninga sidings.

Steam adventures at Pichi Richi for children from seven to seventy.

The Pichi Richi tourist train runs from the old station at Quorn

The railway station at Hawker lives on – as a restaurant.

The Pichi Richi railway Society runs a tourist line in the Flinders Ranges, maintaining a railway presence in the town of Quorn, long by-passed when the broad gauge went through. If you know where to look, you can find some strange signs carved into the stone bridges along the Quorn line. Chinese workers were brought to Australia to work on railway construction, amid much union and political opposition, and Chinese characters carved into the stone bridges record the names of the masons who built them.

Another railway heritage society is based in Peterborough, S.A., maintaining a railway museum and offering tourist rides.

Finally, the Port Dock museum in Port Adelaide has a huge collection of locomotives and cars.

The problems of maintaining a steam railway thirty or forty years after the end of the steam age presents problems known only to the owners of vintage cars. There are no storehouses of spare parts for ancient steam engines. Far-sighted preservationists bought up big at railway auctions late in the

Steam nostalgia at Peterborough

steamtime, but who could predict what their needs would be? The unlimited enthusiasm which keeps steam power alive at Pichi Richi and Alice Downs, and at a score of other locations across Australia, is underpinned by a dwindling resource of expertise in engineering, boilermaking, steam fitting and plain ingenuity that keeps these old wheels rolling.

The partnership of steam power and Australia's outback railways was not a happy one. Neither of the two simple needs of the steam engine, good coal and good water, existed anywhere along the lines and had to be carried in, sometimes for hundreds of miles. Where water was available, from underground sources, it was often of such poor quality that boiler damage accounted for 90 percent of the maintenance costs of locomotive operation. It could all have been avoided if the politicians of the day had taken the advice of a far-sighted engineer they had employed, the Englishman Henry Deane.

Deane had come to Australia in 1906 to build the 'impossible railway', a 50 km long mining line accessing a coal and oil shale deposit in a deep valley of the

Blue Mountains in New South Wales. His Wolgan Valley railway was a triumph of engineering and of manual labour. Almost entirely without construction machinery, using the muscles of horse and man and the power of dynamite, Deane ran his first train along the completed winding and precipitous track less than a year after his first surveys.

Hired then as Chief Engineer for the Trans-Continental railway project, Henry Deane warned the Federal Government well before the first trains ran that there would be big problems caused by water quality. And he told the Government of a then new idea in railway locomotive power emerging in Europe. It involved the coupling of one of Dr Rudolf Diesel's ingenious engines to an electric generator, in turn supplying electrical power to motors that hauled the load.

But the powers of Government knew only the steam engine. Perhaps it was all they could understand, certainly both the diesel engine, and electricity itself, were concepts beyond their imaginations. Deane's proposal was rejected out of hand. His disappointment was one of the factors behind his subsequent resignation. It was to be thirty-six years before the first diesel-electric locomotive ran on the transcontinental, and within a very few years of that, steam had gone entirely.

Today's diesel-electric locomotives hauling the Ghan and the other passenger and freight trains of Australian National are the products of a design partnership between the railway and locomotive builders. AN's unique needs have created a stable of unique locomotives. In recent years, the opening at Whyalla of a locomotive re-building plant by the American company Morrison- Knudsen has made new locomotives out of old, extending the life and vastly improving the performance of an earlier generation of AN's diesels.

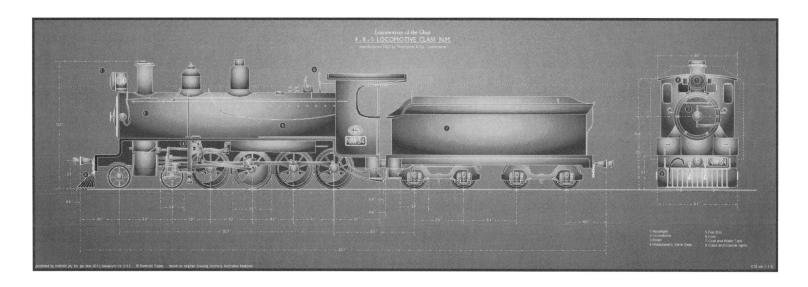

Locomotives of the Ghan

The Ghan of the steam era, The Original Ghan, was hauled almost exclusively by Class NM locomotives, a 1920 design from the Queensland Railways known there as the C17 Class. (Queensland retained throughout the steam era the odd practice of classifying locomotives according to their cylinder diameters. The C17 therefore hat 17-inch cylinders. The practice led to one Queensland type being known as the BB18¼ Class, a terminology rare in world railways.)

The C17's as ordered by the Commonwealth Railways in 1925 from the Castlemaine, Victoria, works of Thompson & Co.

were of 4-9-0 type, with a four-wheel leading bogie and eight driving wheels of 3'9" diameter. So successful were they in Queensland that 227 were built there over more than thirty years.

Commonwealth Railways had taken over the Port Augusta-Oodnadatta line in 1911 as the first stage of the never-realised railway to Darwin, and when in need of new locomotives chose the Queensland design, renamed NM Class. Twenty-two were built in Castlemaine between June 1925 and December 1927. One of the original NM class, NM34, is preserved at the Port Dock Railway Museum at Port Adelaide.

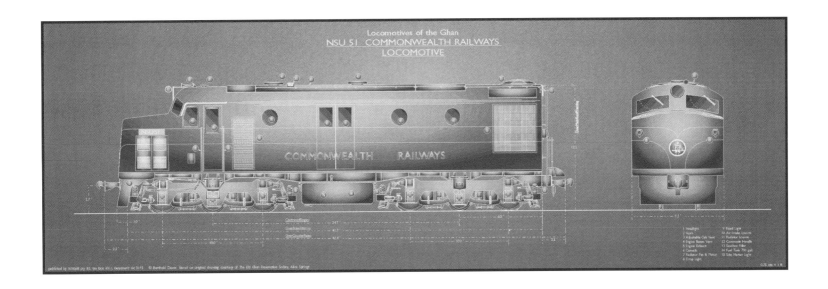

Locomotives of the Ghan
NSU 51 COMMONWEALTH RAILWAYS
LOCOMOTIVE

Almost forty years after the Trans Australia Railway Chief Engineer Henry Deane's rejected suggestion that diesel-electric locomotives should be investigated by Commonwealth Railways, the first diesels were ordered for the Ghan Line, and the withdrawal of the gallant old NM's parallel deliveries of the new locomotives from builders in England. They were classed as NSU, and in June 1954 two of them hauled the first diesel Ghan to Alice Springs.

The second generation of diesel-electric power came in 1965 with the NT class. Sulzer powered like the NSU's, but built in Australia by Tulloch Ltd, the NT class worked the Ghan until the more powerful NJ class diesels arrived from Clyde Engineering in 1971.

The six NJ's incorporated much of what Commonwealth Railways and Clyde Engineering had learned together about diesel-electric operations in harsh conditions on the Trans-Australia Line, and these locomotives were to serve well until the narrow gauge line to The Alice was superseded by the new standard gauge via Tarcoola in 1980. With much life left in them, they

2nd class coach at Quorn

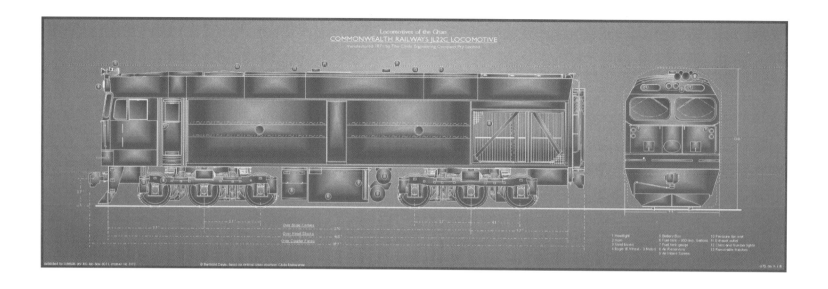

Locomotives of the Ghan
COMMONWEALTH RAILWAYS JL22C LOCOMOTIVE
manufactured 1971 by The Clyde Engineering Company Pty Limited

were transferred to other narrow gauge operations of Australian National.

With the standard gauge came the integration of the railway to Alice Springs with the trans-continental operations of Australian National, and the AN locomotive fleet was available to haul the Ghan. AN, and its predecessor Commonwealth Railways, had developed expertise in collaborating with locomotive builders to provide the best power for the job the railway faced.

The coming of the American railway engineering specialists Morrison-Knudsen, who built a locomotive reconditioning and up-dating plant at Whyalla, South Australia, brought to The Ghan re-built locomotives designed for the Central Australia run. Classed CLP, they combine the classic lines of the General Motors 'E' series bodies of the 1950's with mechanical, electrical and electronic systems of the 1990's and beyond, and they are the power of the Ghan's future.

The future

Australian National, an innovator in an industry unfortunately lacking in innovation, is determined that its creation, The Ghan, will remain a feature of the Australian tourist industry. Almost uniquely among Australian railways, Australian National has made its passenger services pay their way. Its northbound Ghans average 75–80% bookings year round, southbound is less successful.

The Ghan's passengers come from around the world, but surveys show that about half of them come from the State of Victoria. Will the Ghan extend then to Melbourne? Maybe,

End of story? The future of the Ghan seems to lie in the stars. 1335 km long and crossing one of the harshest regions in the world to connect a small Outback town of 28,000 with excellent air connections to the rest of the country, makes the Ghan a very unlikely enterprise. Australian National says it even runs paying its way, which being fairly unique in the world of railways makes it even more astonishing.

Australian National says, now that a standard gauge line runs from Melbourne to Adelaide. But in the immediate future, Australian National's plan for The Ghan is to confirm its place in the Central Australian tourist industry, and to help develop southbound traffic of tourists to balance the northbound trade.

On board, AN aims to improve the level of service which already meets and exceeds all but the most indulgent – and expensive – offerings of railways anywhere. The Legendary Ghan, the train to Outback Australia, will remain one of the Great Railway Journeys of the World.

Thank you

A great many people helped during the making of *The Ghan*. We wish to thank the following persons or organisations – and especially those we forgot to mention:

Adelaide: Ron Fluck, Port Dock Museum; Christina Holmdahl, Australian National; Bob Sampson, Australian National; Steve Yorke, Port Dock Museum;

Port Augusta: Peter McGever, Australian National; Marion Ellis, Australian National; Ambrose Lyons, Port Pirie; Ron Davey, Australian National, Bryan Stewart, Australian National;

Tarcoola: Rolly St.Clair;

Alice Springs: Noel Fullerton, Virginia Camel Farm; Panorama Guth; Old Ghan Preservation Society; Collin Phillis, Australian National;

Marree: Reg Dodds, Marree Arabunna Peoples Committee; The Marree Hotel;

And: Elizabeth's Australian Designer Jewellery, Southgate, Melbourne, Vic; Robert Oberdorfer, Desert Gems, Southgate, Melbourne, Vic; Michael Peter, Clyde Engineering, Granville, NSW; Colin Workman, Peterborough, SA; and anybody we forgot to mention.

The Authors

Jim Downes worked for 35 years as a newspaper and broadcast journalist. For almost half that time he was a reporter of national and international affairs for the television program *4 Corners*, and for the last two years of his ABC career was presenter for *Countrywide*. Jim lives now in country New South Wales and works as a freelance writer and narrator. He is author of the book *A Big Country*.

Berthold Daum lives in Melbourne. Originally a computer scientist, he now works as a freelance photographer - and still spends most of the time behind a computer screen. His photography has won national and international awards. He published the books *Animus* and *Bushnights*.

Christine Stevens lives in Sydney and is an expert on the Australian Muslim population. She is author of the book *Tin Mosques and 'Ghan towns*.

Dick Kimber lives in Alice Springs and is a writer-historian, the author of *Man from Arltunga* and many articles on central Australian history.

Margaret Mackay, a freelance photographer, writer and publisher, lives in Coober Pedy and has published *Coober Pedy - the next generation*.